Koala Bears

Eliza Robbins

Rosen Classroom Books & Materials
New York

1

A koala has gray or brown fur.

A koala also has some white fur.

A baby koala holds its mom's fur.

A koala climbs trees.

A koala eats leaves from trees.

A koala sleeps in the daytime.

Words to Know

gray

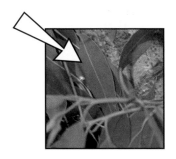

leaves